BEGIN WITH A BLANKET
creative play for infants

by Rachel Coley, MS, OT/L

Published by CanDo Kiddo, LLC

What do you DO with a newborn when he's awake, fed, and not crying?

How do you PLAY with a floppy, squishy baby in her first weeks of life?

What baby gear is best to help your little one LEARN and GROW?

Believe it or not, babies are born ready to move and play. The best kept secret in parenting is that you don't need to fill your home with expensive baby gear to keep your baby happy and to help him learn and grow. In fact, the overuse of "baby holding devices" - bouncy seats, baby swings, car seat carriers and other infant positioners - decreases movement and play during the critical developmental period of the first months of life.

As a pediatric Occupational Therapist I've seen and treated the effects of decreased early movement - upper body and core muscle weakness, decreased coordination, sensory processing problems, head flattening and more. I'm here to spread the word that many of these are preventable. And it all begins with a blanket...

In this book, I'll show you simple play activities to get your baby out of restrictive baby gear in the first months of life and help build lifelong cognitive, sensory and motor skills.

Happy Playing!

Rachel

ABOUT THE AUTHOR

Rachel Coley, MS, OT/L, is a licensed Occupational Therapist with over 10 years of experience working exclusively with children and 4 of those years specifically with infants and toddlers. She has advanced specialized training in infant neurodevelopment, sensory processing, Torticollis and Plagiocephaly (infant neck and head shape issues). Rachel has participated in research and humanitarian projects related to the extreme deprivation of early movement and play in Romanian orphanages.

Rachel lives in Charlotte, North Carolina, with her husband, two kids and wonderdog. She enjoys mountain biking, whitewater kayaking and teaching and practicing yoga.

Follow the blog at **CanDoKiddo.com** and join the conversation on the **CanDo Kiddo Facebook page** at facebook.com/candokiddo.

BONUS MATERIALS

In addition to the activities in this book, I'd like to share a collection of free bonus materials with you:

- A sneak peek of 5 activities from the next book in this series, *Simple Play: Easy Fun For Babies.* This book offers 40 activities for sitters, crawlers, cruisers and standers.

- Printable onesie stickers featuring 19 adorable milestones of the first year to document your kiddo's growth and development

- A printable Tummy Time Tracker Tool

- Printable Black & White Baby Play Cards

To receive your bonus materials, simply visit

www.candokiddo.com/bonus

or scan this QR code from your mobile device

YOUR BABY'S TIMELINE

Instead of specific months and weeks of a newborn's life, the timeline of activities in this book is easily modified to match your newborn's development.

Try PART ONE activities when your baby...

is quiet and still with some small arm and leg movements

does a lot of looking

mainly keeps one cheek on the blanket in Tummy Time

requires full head support when held

Try PART TWO activities when your baby...

begins to briefly lift head and look forward in Tummy Time

straightens arms and legs briefly

makes faster and larger movements

Try PART THREE activities when your baby...

holds her head up in Tummy Time for at least 5 seconds

opens her hands & kicks her legs

watches your face

Try PART FOUR activities when your baby...

keeps head lifted in Tummy Time for at least 30 seconds

brings hands to mouth

opens and closes hands

DISCLAIMER

Having a newborn means being vigilant. All CanDo Kiddo activities are designed for CLOSE supervision. That means an adult within arms reach with eyes on baby.

Some CanDo Kiddo activities include household or non-toy items that could be ingested or become strangulation hazards. Please use your own judgement with your child. Again, CLOSE supervision is required to keep baby safe. CanDo Kiddo, LLC, is not liable for any injury incurred while replicating any activity found within this book.

Always remember that you won't know that your baby can roll, put toys in her mouth, or push herself over a Tummy Time pillow until she does. No timeline of expected milestones can ensure safety - only CLOSE supervision can.

Rachel Coley is a licensed Occupational Therapist. Any advice in this book is not a replacement for medical advice from a physician. Please consult your child's pediatrician if you suspect any medical or developmental issues with your child. These tips do not replace the relationship between therapist and client in a one on one treatment session with an individualized treatment plan based on their professional evaluation.

PART ONE

TABLETOP TUMMY TIME

Tummy Time should begin in the first week for healthy, full-term infants. But HOW?! Newborns see and are most interested in faces, so put baby on her blanket on a tabletop to help you get right up close to those sleepy eyes. Face-to-face Tummy Time also lets your little one see, smell and feel that you're near.

She won't be able to fully lift her head yet, but all of her efforts to do so are building neck and back muscles. Belly-down play helps baby's muscles and joints stretch out of her fetal position. In the first weeks, aim for 1-5 minute bursts of Tummy Time frequently throughout the day.

Never walk away from baby on a tabletop. Newborns can reflexively roll as a survival instinct when face-down, even in the first days of life.

BENEFITS: neck strength, upper body strength, spinal development, pressure & stretch sense, sense of touch, visual sense, body awareness, socialization & bonding, stretch & strengthen out of womb position, prevent Flat Head Syndrome.

See the Glossary of Terms at the end of this book for technical terminology of benefits listed.

SIDELYING MIRROR PLAY

A sidelying position for play varies the pressure on your baby's skull to help prevent Flat Head Syndrome (Positional Plagiocephaly). It also helps baby bring hands together - an important developmental task. Sidelying makes leg movements easier in the early weeks by reducing the effect of gravity and also helps baby begin to balance the strength of her belly-side muscles (flexors) and back-side muscles (extensors).

Babies are fascinated by seeing themselves in a mirror - even in the first days of life. Simple looking activities, such as mirror play, help your newborn develop attention and concentration.

To support baby in the sidelying position, roll a towel into a log shape 3-5" in diameter and tuck it under the blanket to keep it in place. Lay your little one with back against the towel roll, alternating which side of your baby's body and head are on the floor each time you put him in sidelying.

BENEFITS: spinal development, pressure & stretch sense, sense of touch, movement sense, visual sense, body awareness, attention, stretch & strengthen out of womb position, bring hands together, prevent Flat Head Syndrome, leg strength, core strength

NAKED PLAYTIME

Letting your baby spend time in her birthday suit is great for preventing diaper rash and for sensory development - WIN, WIN! Without clothes, your little one's skin will experience a much richer interaction with the world around her. What looks like lying on the floor and wiggling is actually your baby learning how her body relates to the ground beneath her through touch and her pressure & stretch sense. This wiggly floortime lays the foundation for the motor milestones to come - rolling, sitting, standing and walking. Your kiddo can enjoy naked playtime in belly-up, sidelying and Tummy Time positions.

Without planning, naked time can get messy! Use bed pads for incontinence ("pee pads") to keep your baby's blanket clean and dry. Drape a cloth diaper loosely over boy parts to keep your walls, ceilings and shirt dry.

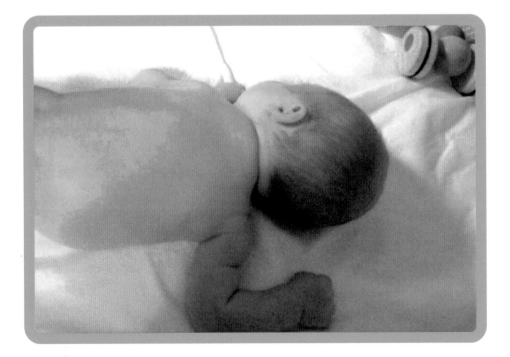

BENEFITS: sense of touch, pressure & stretch sense, body awareness, stretch & strengthen out of womb position

RIDE AN IMAGINARY BICYCLE

Your baby has spent months growing in the fetal position - with spine rounded and arms and legs folded against the body. One of the first physical tasks of the newborn is to stretch and strengthen out of that fetal position. Most "baby holding devices" - bouncy chairs, baby swings, car seat carriers and other infant positioners - support infants with a curved back and flexed hips and shoulders. This inhibits the early motor milestones of stretching and strengthening out of the womb position.

Limit your newborn's time in "baby holding devices" to two hours per day or less. elp gently stretch his hips and legs by pedaling your little one's feet as if he is riding a tiny imaginary bicycle while laying on his back. He'll gain valuable awareness of his body through your touch and his sense of muscles and joints moving. Try moving his legs slowly, quickly, backward and forward. Take advantage of the face-to-face time offered by this belly-up activity by talking or singing to your baby.

BENEFITS: spinal development, pressure & stretch sense, visual sense, body awareness, socialization & bonding, stretch & strengthen out of womb position, leg strength

PRACTICE HOLDING HEAD UP

Newborns are stronger than we give them credit for. With support, your baby can (and should) practice holding her head up in the first weeks of life. Being upright helps her develop awareness of her position in space. This position promotes integration of the movement sense and the visual sense.

With fingers spread wide, sandwich your baby's upper chest in your two hands. Support the back of the head lightly with the index and middle fingers of the hand on baby's back. Cradle baby's chin in the web-space (between your thumb and index finger) of your front hand. This position allows you to prevent any dramatic head dropping but gives your wee one the freedom to lift and even turn her bobblehead, gaining valuable opportunities for neck strengthening and stretching.

BENEFITS: spinal development, neck strength, movement sense, visual sense, body awareness, socialization & bonding, stretch & strengthen out of womb position, prevent Flat Head Syndrome

LOTION MASSAGE

The touch sense is reportedly the most developed at birth, and the skin is the largest of your newborn's organs. The sense of smell is the most directly connected to the emotion center of her brain. Use both senses to connect with your little one by putting an essential oil on your wrists while massaging baby with her favorite baby lotion. She can smell the gentle scent from your skin while she enjoys your touch. Newborn skin is sensitive, so avoid putting essential oils directly on your baby. Stores and individuals who sell essential oils can guide you toward specific scents that are calming and those that are alerting.

Slowly massage your baby's feet, legs, body and arms. Avoid getting lotion on your infant's hands since those may touch the face, mouth, and eyes. Gently stretch baby's joints as you go.

Don't feel limited to after bathtime for lotion massages, when your kiddo may be too tired, cold or hungry to enjoy a massage. A lotion massage is a great playtime activity.

BENEFITS: sense of touch, pressure & stretch sense, sense of smell, body awareness, socialization & bonding, stretch & strengthen out of womb position

A BAG OF RICE FOR TUMMY TIME

Most babies resist tummy time because it's hard work! In the first month, your little one's legs will still be bent and flexed toward her body, pushing more weight towards her large head. The whole thing winds up being equivalent to an Olympic powerlifting session.

One simple way to help is to anchor your baby's hips with a little additional weight. You can use your hand, but that may limit your ability to play or get in a face-to-face position with your kiddo. Try placing a 1 pound bag of rice on the low back and rump area to give you a hands-free solution to tummy time woes.

Aim to give your baby 30 minutes of tummy time a day by the end of month one. This will likely take many, many (many) short periods of belly-down play. Try placing your baby on her tummy after each diaper change.

BENEFITS: spinal development, pressure & stretch sense, sense of touch, body awareness, stretch & strengthen out of womb position, prevent Flat Head Syndrome, upper body strength, core strength, neck strength

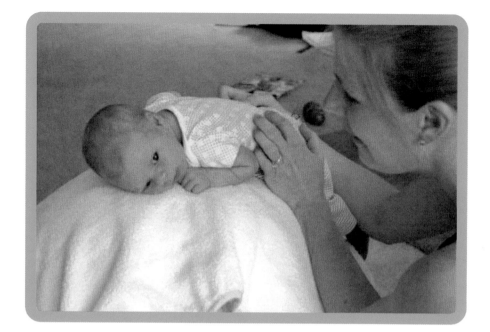

ROLLING ON AN EXERCISE BALL

Your baby's movement sense began developing in utero as you went about your daily activities. Now it's time for baby to experience movement outside of the womb. She'll combine information from her movement sense with her visual and pressure & stretch senses to learn about her body position related to gravity. This integration of multiple senses is important for the development of sensory processing skills. These are the means by which we respond to the information our body is receiving from the environment.

Rolling your little one on a ball is a more valuable experience for sensory development than putting her in a soft, supportive infant swing because it affords her the freedom of movement to respond to what she sees and feels. You may see her look more awake, try to lift her head or move her arms and legs when belly-down on a ball. Don't have an exercise ball? Try rolling baby gently over your thighs while belly-down on your lap.

BENEFITS: movement sense, pressure & stretch sense, sense of touch, spinal development, visual sense, body awareness, socialization & bonding, stretch & strengthen out of womb position, prevent Flat Head Syndrome, upper body strength, core strength, neck strength

BLACK & WHITE PICTURE PLAY

In the first weeks of life, your newborn's vision is limited but developing. Babies are color-blind and near-sighted at birth and attend best to simple, high contrast images located 6 to 18 inches from their face.

Activity gyms offer valuable playtime out of "baby holding devices" for baby to stretch, strengthen and learn about his body and how it relates to his new surroundings. Many activity gyms are visually cluttered with hang-down toys and covered with busy patterned fabric. They may overwhelm your infant in the critical first weeks of visual development. Reduce the distractions by removing toys from your baby's gym and taping simple black and white picture cards in various positions to encourage head turning. Printable black and white pictures are available in the CanDo Kiddo Etsy shop (candokiddo.etsy.com).

BENEFITS: visual sense, eye movement skills, neck strength, spinal development, pressure & stretch sense, body awareness, attention, stretch & strengthen out of womb position, upper body strength, leg strength

WARM & COOL COTTON BALLS

Because newborns in the first weeks of life are just "waking up" to the world around them, sometimes just experiencing new sensations and remaining alert and content for a period of time is valuable play. Your little one won't be doing much reaching or grabbing in the first month, so she'll be dependent on you to bring new touch experiences to her. Alternate dipping cotton balls in bowls of warm and cool water and touching them to baby's face and body. Watch her facial expressions, body position, and even her breathing respond to these new touch sensations.

Given your infant's strength and abilities in the first four weeks of life, "Baby Holding Devices" typically limit her to only using her visual and sometimes movement senses (in the case of swings and bouncy seats). These devices promote passive sensory experiences with restricted opportunity to respond actively with movement. By limiting your infant's time in "Baby Holding Devices" and giving her a wide variety of sensory experiences through play, you're helping her learn and grow.

BENEFITS: touch sense, pressure & stretch sense, body awareness, socialization & bonding

A MOBILE ABOVE BABY'S BLANKET

Most nursery mobiles are designed to go over baby's crib. But looking and watching are play activities for your little one in his first weeks of life. Look for a mobile that you can hang over baby's play spot. Watching a mobile move slowly helps your newborn develop attention as well as visual skills while stretching and strengthening on his blanket. Hang the mobile low enough for baby to have to turn his head to look at its different objects.

Try to find a mobile with high contrast objects that are oriented towards the baby instead of towards an adult in the room. You can use an inexpensive photo mobile to create a custom mobile, using its photo clips to hang pictures, paper crafts, balloons and more.

BENEFITS: attention, visual sense, eye movement skills, neck strength, stretch & strengthen out of womb position, spinal development, prevent Flat Head Syndrome

PART TWO

FLOATING BATH TOY

Thanks to the stretching and strengthening of Tummy Time in month one, your baby is beginning to be able to lift her head slightly to briefly look at objects on the floor a few inches in front of her. Novelty goes a long way when it comes to Tummy Time tolerance. Floating a bath toy in a shallow pan of water will give your little one something new and exciting to watch. Bump the toy to make it move and watch your baby move her eyes and head to try to follow. If your newborn gets cranky, give her a break in your lap or on her back before trying again.

<u>Always</u> keep your eyes on your baby near water. Babies can drown in even a shallow pan of water.

BENEFITS: spinal development, pressure & stretch sense, sense of touch, visual sense, eye movement skills, attention, stretch & strengthen out of womb position, prevent Flat Head Syndrome, upper body strength, core strength, neck strength

A STREAMER CURTAIN

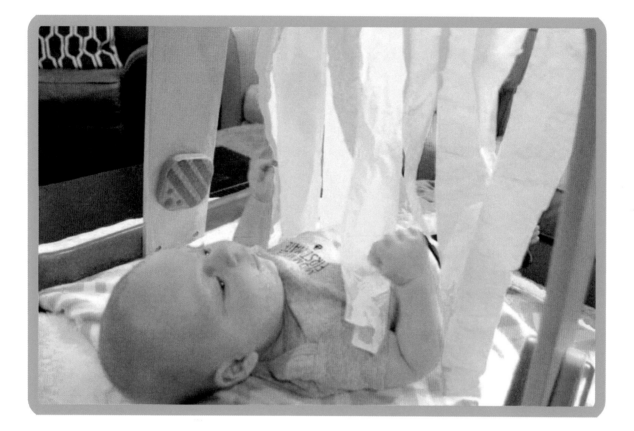

Your little one is beginning to realize that his movements can have an effect on the world around him - what fun! He's gotten strong enough to move his limbs against gravity, and he's stretched his joints enough to straighten his arms and legs - making month two full of wiggling.

Take advantage of the fact that your newborn isn't yet consistently grasping by hanging streamers from his activity gym for him to touch. You can substitute strips of wrapping tissue paper for crepe streamers. They'll both make a nice crinkly sound when touched. Your infant will get both touch and sound feedback from his movements and learn from the cause and effect of his actions.

BENEFITS: sense of touch, hearing sense, visual sense, body awareness, attention, pressure & stretch sense, stretch & strengthen out of womb position, upper body strength, coordination of reach

GIFT BAG TUMMY TIME

Sometimes the bag a baby gift came in is as much fun as the gift inside! Gift bags with bright bold patterns with contrasting colors will capture your infant's interest. Bags can either stand up independently or be hung by their handles from the knobs of a cabinet or dresser to be gazed at in Tummy Time.

Variety is often the key to keeping your baby interested, so try changing the bag when your infant gets fussy in Tummy Time before you take a break from the position altogether. Aim for at least 60 minutes of Tummy Time daily by the end of month two split into many shorter increments.

If your baby still hates Tummy Time, try waiting at least 30 minutes after a feeding for this play position. Sometimes belly-down play can be uncomfortable on a full tummy or exacerbate spit-ups.

BENEFITS: spinal development, pressure & stretch sense, sense of touch, body awareness, stretch & strengthen out of womb position, prevent Flat Head Syndrome, upper body strength, core strength, neck strength

SIDELYING WITH BOOKS

As your baby's vision matures, you'll likely notice her increasing interest in faces and pictures. This makes books more interesting to your growing newborn. Look for books with high contrast images or real photographs of faces and objects, as these best match your baby's visual and cognitive abilities in month two.

Sidelying continues to be a vital position for giving your baby a variety of positions throughout the day - important for motor development. By month two, your little one benefits from the opportunity to experience accidental rolling resulting from her movements in sidelying. Try sidelying without a rolled towel for some of your baby's playtime.

Sidelying is also a beneficial play position for preventing head flattening. Check your newborn's head shape from above every few days - dividing the top of your infant's head into 4 quadrants with imaginary lines from ear to ear and nose to back of skull. Do the quadrants look even and symmetrical? If you notice flattening on one side, make a point to place your baby in sidelying for play more on the side opposite the flattening. Flattening that is not improving by your baby's **two month checkup** should be evaluated by a physical or occupational therapist specializing in infant head and neck issues to identify possible causes and help you modify baby's environment and play to correct her head shape.

BENEFITS: spinal development, pressure & stretch sense, sense of touch, visual sense, body awareness, attention, stretch & strengthen out of womb position, bring hands together, prevent Flat Head Syndrome

TUMMY TIME PILLOW READING

Another great way for your baby to experience books in month two is to use a Tummy Time pillow, nursing pillow or other firm pillow under her chest. Raising her upper body higher than her lower body makes head lifting easier and may increase Tummy Time tolerance. The pillow also gives a soft spot for resting as needed, which may increase your infant's overall time on her belly.

Most babies are born with slight muscle imbalances from being curled up in the womb. When you place your infant in supportive "baby holding devices" in a semi-reclined position, gravity tends to pull your newborn into her preferred womb position, exacerbating these imbalances. This is often seen with neck tightness resulting in head flattening on one side. Freedom of movement in a variety of positions is the natural way for babies to stretch and strengthen any asymmetries and, in most cases, avoid the need for therapies or helmets. Minimize your baby's time in semi-reclined positioners by providing lots of playtime on her blanket and varying her position, as with Tummy Time pillow reading.

BENEFITS: spinal development, neck strength, upper body strength, core strength, pressure & stretch sense, visual sense, body awareness, attention, stretch & strengthen out of womb position, prevent Flat Head Syndrome

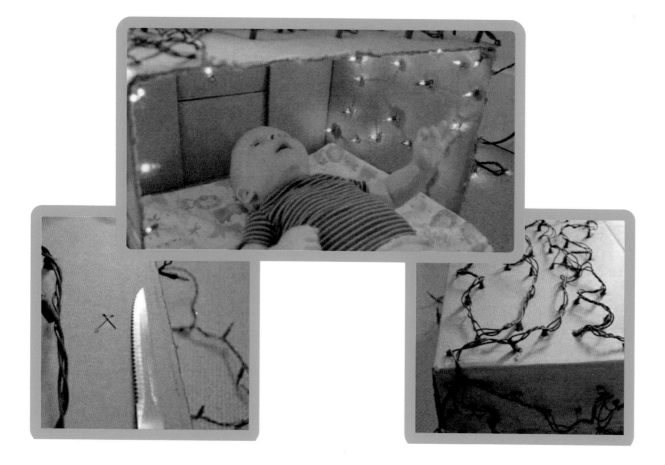

A STARGAZING BOX

A Stargazing Box takes a little prep work but is a great go-to for a hard to entertain baby or a particularly fussy day. Find the biggest box possible so that your little one can move and stretch without getting scratched by the lights. Cut small X's in the sides of the box and poke Christmas lights through to shine inside the box. A large enough box will accommodate belly-up play as well as sidelying and Tummy Time positions.

If you've noticed that your baby prefers to turn her head in one direction or if your newborn has a flat spot, place lights strategically only on sides of the box that encourage head turning in the non-preferred direction or toward the non-flat side.

BENEFITS: spinal development, pressure & stretch sense, visual sense, body awareness, attention, stretch & strengthen out of womb position, prevent Flat Head Syndrome, neck strength

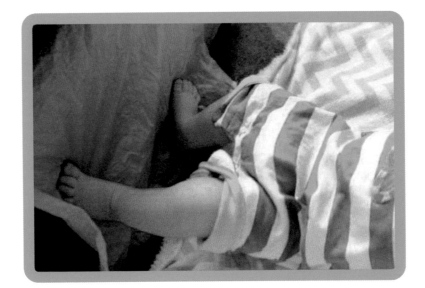

TISSUE PAPER KICKING

Newborns gain valuable awareness of their own body in month two by moving and observing responses to that movement. Help your infant continue to stretch and strengthen out of her womb position and learn about her feet and legs during belly-up play with tissue paper. Your little one will have to master lifting her legs and engaging her belly muscles in order to roll, so all the kicking you'll see in months two and three is paving the way for a much bigger milestone! She'll get the added feedback of feeling and hearing the tissue paper to help learn that her actions have an effect. Your baby will also strengthen the muscles of her neck as she looks down toward her feet as she hears and feels crinkly tissue paper under her toes.

Position baby's blanket near a couch. Tuck a sheet or two of wrapping tissue under the couch cushions so they drape down to the floor. Scoot baby close so that those little feet can kick and rustle the paper.

BENEFITS: leg strength, core strength, stretch & strengthen out of womb position, attention, body awareness, hearing sense, sense of touch, pressure & stretch sense, spinal development, eye movement skills

SOUND LOCALIZING

Did you know that even in the first weeks of life newborns can turn their heads toward sounds and follow sounds that move from one side of their head to the other? This is called sound localization, and play with this skill can help your little one tune into his hearing sense and stretch and strengthen neck muscles.

In a quiet room with your baby belly-up on his blanket or propped on your lap, play soft music from a portable device on one side of your infant's head. Give him time to respond and watch for the reaction of his eyes and head as he tries to find the sound. After several minutes, move the music to his other side and wait for a response. Continue the game as long as your baby is quiet, alert and interested.

BENEFITS: spinal development, neck strength, movement sense, visual sense, body awareness, socialization & bonding, stretch & strengthen out of womb position, prevent Flat Head Syndrome

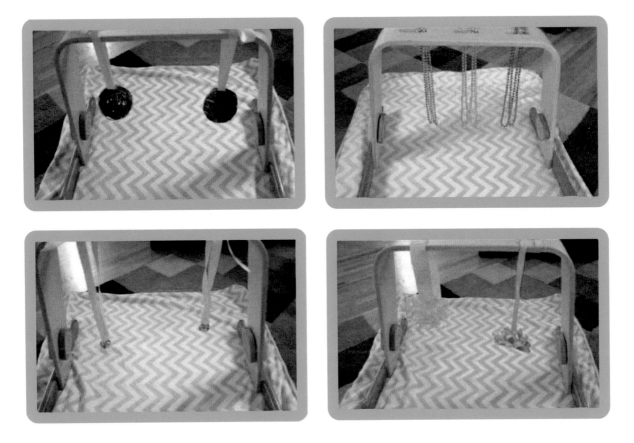

TOYS HUNG FROM ACTIVITY GYM

Babies are careful watchers of the world around them, but your little one also needs plenty of active playtime with people and objects in his environment. Around month two, you'll see him swing his arms and - through repetition - learn that he can intentionally touch objects hanging above him. He'll begin to relate how an object looks to how it feels and sounds.

Don't feel limited to the toys that came with your baby's gym - use ribbon or plastic toy links to secure bells, windchimes, beads, textured balls, gift bows and anything else that can be securely attached. Closely supervise your baby's play to make sure that no items break free and become a choking hazard.

BENEFITS: coordination of reach, upper body strength, stretch and strengthen out of womb position, visual sense, eye movement skills, sense of touch, pressure & stretch sense, spinal development

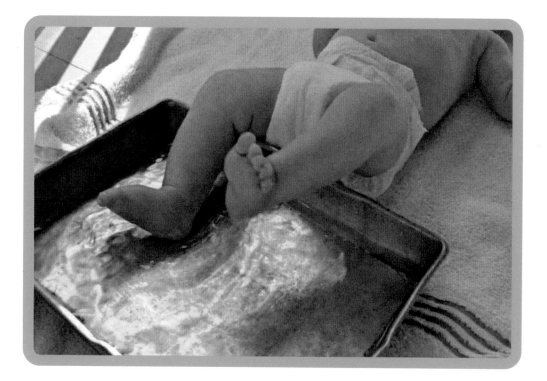

WATER KICKING

In just a few short weeks, your newborn has progressed from just beginning to move the weight of his legs against gravity to kicking like crazy! Kicking is important work for the development of leg and belly muscles, but your baby just thinks it's just fun. With a shallow pan of water placed under his feet, your kiddo will feel and hear new sensations as he kicks. Through repetition he'll learn that his his movements are causing all the splashing.

You'll likely notice that your baby kicks each leg individually much of the time, similar to the leg movements of walking. The brain is wired for alternating movements and it's important to give your newborn opportunities to keep practicing them in anticipation of walking, running, bicycle riding and more.

BENEFITS: leg strength, core strength, stretch & strengthen out of womb position, attention, body awareness, hearing sense, sense of touch, pressure & stretch sense, spinal development

BABY PULL-UPS

Before babies develop fine motor (hand and finger) skills, they lay the foundation by building upper body strength in the first months of life through movement and play. Baby Pull-Ups help your newborn prepare for school success years from now.

Prop your infant against your thighs or a pillow. Let him grasp your thumbs in his hands as you wrap your other four fingers around each of his forearms. Give a very gentle, slight pull on both arms. Look for him to

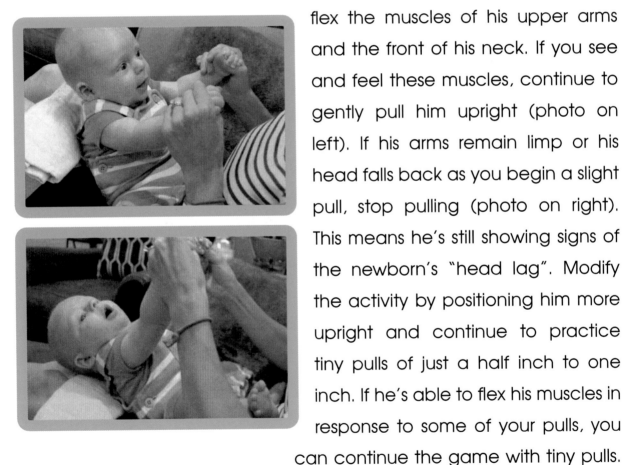

flex the muscles of his upper arms and the front of his neck. If you see and feel these muscles, continue to gently pull him upright (photo on left). If his arms remain limp or his head falls back as you begin a slight pull, stop pulling (photo on right). This means he's still showing signs of the newborn's "head lag". Modify the activity by positioning him more upright and continue to practice tiny pulls of just a half inch to one inch. If he's able to flex his muscles in response to some of your pulls, you can continue the game with tiny pulls.

If he isn't showing any muscle response to your gentle pulls, stop the game and try again in a week or two.

BENEFITS: neck strength, upper body strength, core strength, grasping skills, hand strength, spinal development, body awareness, pressure & stretch sense, movement sense, touch sense, visual sense, socialization & bonding, prevent Flat Head Syndrome

PART THREE

FRESH HERBS TOUCHING PAN

Somewhere around month three your newborn will likely go through a magical time when her hands open up and explore but she hasn't quite mastered grasping objects and putting them in her mouth. Take advantage of this brief time with touching pans. Fresh herbs make a great touching pan because they also expose your baby to new smells.

Tummy Time on a Tummy Time pillow, nursing pillow or belly-down over your thighs make great positions to explore touch pans before your baby can reach with one hand in Tummy Time. When your baby gets tired or fussy, try continuing the touching activity with your little one in your lap.

Be sure to wash those little hands after playing with fresh herbs to remove the plant oils so that they aren't later rubbed on the face or eyes.

BENEFITS: sense of touch, sense of smell, visual sense, grasping skills, coordination of reach, spinal development, pressure & stretch sense, attention, stretch & strengthen out of womb position, bring hands together, prevent Flat Head Syndrome, upper body strength, neck strength, core strength, hand strength

MOUTH WAKE UP

In the early weeks, newborn noises are usually pretty limited...to crying. But as your little one grows and gets more active, you'll hear him begin vocal play as he gains awareness of his mouth. Although he's not ready for the oral stimulation of food in month three, you can use a damp washcloth to "wake up" his mouth and give him valuable sensations that help him learn about his lips, cheeks, tongue, gums and palate.

With a damp washcloth over your index finger, gently wipe your infant's gums, inner cheeks, tongue and the front of the roof of his mouth. This helps your baby's brain become more aware of these parts. Then stick out your tongue and watch for your baby to try to do the same. Tap or wipe his tongue with the washcloth to help him sense his own body. Pop your lips, puff your cheeks and make a variety of mouth positions and see if he'll try to imitate.

BENEFITS: body awareness, speech, mouth coordination, pressure & stretch sense, sense of touch, visual sense, attention, socialization & bonding

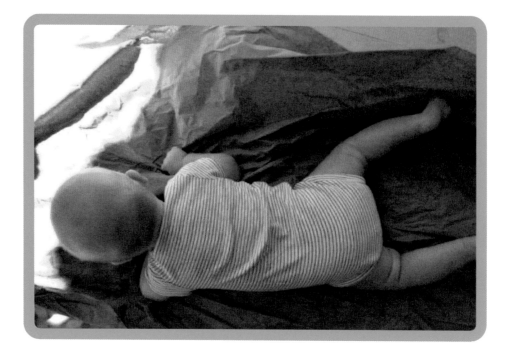

TISSUE PAPER WIGGLE

Give your little one new sensations by placing her on crinkly paper for playtime. Wrapping tissue paper works great, as does crumpled wrapping paper or butcher paper - both of which hold up better if you have a big drooler. In belly-up play, you may see her kick or wiggle, and in Tummy Time you might notice her open her hands to grasp at the paper beneath her.

"Baby Holding Devices" are often over-used because of their convenience for parents. But in the first months of life, captivating your baby's curiosity and attention with new experiences and sensations can provide you with the few "hands free" moments you need while helping your baby to grow and learn. Just be sure to continue closely supervising your little one as she plays. Newborns are inherently interested in nearly everything - it's all new to them - making simple activities like wiggling on crinkly tissue paper exciting.

BENEFITS: body awareness, spinal development, pressure & stretch sense, sense of touch, visual sense, attention, stretch & strengthen out of womb position, prevent Flat Head Syndrome, upper body strength, core strength, neck strength

BALLOON KICKS

For a dollar or two at your local grocery's floral department, you can buy yourself several days of helium balloon fun for your little one! Loosely tie a balloon to each ankle and watch your baby marvel at them dance as he kicks his feet.

By taking a skill that your infant is working on, such as kicking, and combining it with different sensations (touch in water play, sound with tissue paper, and sight with balloons), you help him learn about his actions and his senses.

The first weeks and months of life are a critical window for developing lifelong sensory processing skills that help your child make sense of the world around him. The key to developing these skills is your baby's active interaction with the world around him.

As with all CanDo Kiddo activities, close supervision is required. Never leave your baby alone with balloons and discontinue this activity when your baby can roll or bring toys to his mouth.

BENEFITS: body awareness, spinal development, pressure & stretch sense, sense of touch, visual sense, attention, stretch & strengthen out of womb position, prevent Flat Head Syndrome, upper body strength, core strength, neck strength

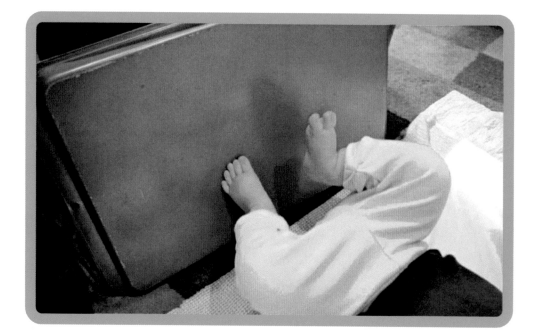

COOKIE SHEET KICKING

This is another activity that draws on your baby's inner drive to kick. Prop a cookie sheet against a couch or chair to let your little one kick loudly. Help your newborn kick a few times to get the idea, if need be. You may find that she will kick the pan placed under her feet in Tummy Time, too!

By giving her novel objects to kick and feel, you draw your newborn's naturally developing interest in her lower body, encourage her to strengthen and set the stage for rolling in the coming weeks. By reducing your infant's time in baby positioners and increasing free play time, you help the natural progression of her motor skills unfold.

Doesn't all this belly-up play make your babies' heads get flat in the back? It would if baby was still on her back. But the freedom of movement she gets lying on her blanket on the floor and activities that promote movement keep the forces on the back of her head changing all the time.

BENEFITS: leg strength, core strength, stretch & strengthen out of womb position, attention, body awareness, hearing sense, sense of touch, pressure & stretch sense, spinal development

BUILD A TOWER, KNOCK IT DOWN

Just because your kiddo is too little to play with blocks himself doesn't mean he can't learn from watching you play with them. Building a small block tower and knocking it down is a great activity to capture your infant's interest in Tummy Time.

Repeated actions such as building and knocking over a small block tower help your baby learn cause and effect. Observing helps him develop attention. And who couldn't use another way to keep your little one happy in Tummy Time?!

Your baby is never too young for speech development. Repeated words that you pair with the repeated actions of building and knocking over lay the foundation for communication. Count the blocks, "one, two, three" or announce, "ready, set, go!" before tower demolition begins.

BENEFITS: visual sense, hearing sense, attention, socialization & bonding, speech, spinal development, pressure & stretch sense, neck strength, core strength,

TOUCH PLAY WITH DRIED BEANS

A touching pan of dried beans is another activity perfect for the few days or weeks when your little one is

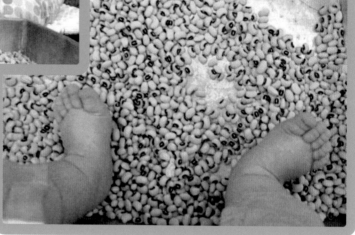

beginning to open his hands but is not yet grasping and bringing things to his mouth. Place a cup or two of dried beans in a metal pan, which gives the beans a nice sound when shifted. Try various positions for play - belly-down over a Tummy Time pillow, seated in your lap or sidelying if you use a low sided pan. Encourage your newborn to touch with hands and give opportunities to touch with feet. Supervise very closely - once your baby is mouthing hands, continue this activity with feet only.

By touching, your baby explores properties of the objects around him - size, shape, weight, texture. By looking and touching, your little one begins to learn to anticipate how things will feel just by looking at them.

BENEFITS: sense of touch, visual sense, hearing sense, pressure & stretch sense, body awareness, attention, coordination of reach, grasping skills, hand strength, neck strength, upper body strength, core strength, spinal development, prevent Flat Head Syndrome, stretch & strengthen out of womb position

MIRROR TUMMY TIME

By now, your baby is getting stronger in Tummy Time and can now look ahead of her for several seconds. Given something new and curious to look at, your infant will work hard to hold that noggin up for even longer. Place baby belly-down in front of a mirror to capture her attention and encourage her to look ahead as long as she can. Aim for 90 minutes of Tummy Time a day by the end of month three.

Notice how your baby begins to use her arms more in Tummy Time during month three. She'll really strengthen arms and shoulders in the weeks ahead. Soon you may notice her arms straightening and elbows lifting briefly off the floor, preparing her muscles to carry her weight in crawling. Crawling is an important motor milestone because it requires alternating movements of both sides of the body - which strengthens the coordination portions of the brain. The strengthening of Tummy Time in the early months helps pave the way for this important movement milestone.

BENEFITS: spinal development, pressure & stretch sense, sense of touch, visual sense, body awareness, attention, stretch & strengthen out of womb position,

BAREFOOT IN THE GRASS

In month three, your baby is beginning to use her hands and mouth to explore through touch. With your help, she can also begin to experience touch through her feet. Getting used to different sensations on her feet will help prepare her for wearing socks and shoes and walking on different textures when she's up and moving on her own.

Help your little one feel the grass under her feet while seated on your lap or while held just above the ground. If your newborn shows distress at the new sensation, give her feet a firm rub or massage. Deep pressure helps calm the brain after the stimulation of light touch from the grass.

BENEFITS: spinal development, pressure & stretch sense, sense of touch, visual sense, body awareness, attention, stretch & strengthen out of womb position,

WATER PLAY WITH HANDS

Combine your newborn's increasing neck strength with his newfound ability to explore with his hands during water play! Use a Tummy Time pillow to support your baby belly-down. Place a shallow pan of water under his hands, offering initial encouragement or help to touch the water if needed.

One facet of sensory processing is the ability to have a normal response to stimuli. Giving your infant lots of opportunities for new touch sensations to be experienced positively in play helps him learn that new feelings aren't scary or yucky. This is the beginning of healthy sensory processing skills that will help your little one when the time comes to touch different foods or get messy with art supplies.

Always keep your eyes on your baby near water. Babies can drown in even a shallow pan of water.

BENEFITS: sense of touch, pressure & stretch sense, visual sense, body awareness, attention, coordination of reach, grasping skills, neck strength, core strength, spinal development, stretch & strengthen out of womb position, bring hands together, prevent Flat Head Syndrome

SIDE-STRETCH DANCE PARTY

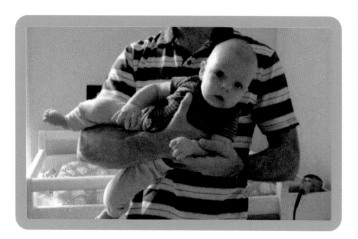

Learning to hold her head up takes more than just neck strength. Your baby has to learn to orient to gravity so that she eventually keeps her head up even when her body is not upright. This will help her to sit and move independently. Given a variety of movement experiences, your newborn uses the movement sensory system of the inner ear and her vision to learn about her body position in relation to the world around her. And you can playfully help!

Hold your baby upright against your chest, facing away from you. Thread your right arm between her legs so that she's sitting on your inner elbow. Wrap your right hand around her left ribcage and gently tip her to the left. Depending on your infant's neck strength and sensory perception, she may hold her head up in this sidelying position. If she needs help, place your left hand gently against the left side of her head for support. Crank up the music and dance as you give your baby a great stretching and strengthening movement experience.

BENEFITS: movement sense, hearing sense, visual sense, pressure & stretch sense, spinal development, neck strength, body awareness, balance, socialization & bonding, stretch & strengthen out of womb position, prevent Flat Head Syndrome

WRIST RATTLES

Make all that arm waving your infant is now doing a little more exciting with soft wrist rattles. This versatile and inexpensive toy will help your little one tune into his hands and promote hand-eye coordination as well as bringing hands together.

Simple movement and play activities with inexpensive and household supplies aren't just great for your newborn - they're convenient for you! Imagine travel without all the baby gear. Just pack your baby's blanket and fill a bright, bold gift bag with tissue paper, a shallow pan for water and touch play, wrist rattles and a board book. You'll have all you need for baby's playtime on the go.

BENEFITS: upper body strength, visual skills, eye movement skills, coordination of reach, bringing hands together, stretch & strengthen out of womb position, body awareness, attention, hearing sense, pressure & stretch sense

PART FOUR

FAMILY PHOTO TUMMY TIME

Taping photos of family members to a baseboard or the lowest part of your wall offers something new and exciting to visually explore in belly-down play. You'll notice your baby getting better at turning her head in this position and beginning to turn her head lo look at the photos.

Tummy Time is not just important for physical development. This position is critical for your baby's growing sensory processing systems, including the movement sense housed in the inner ear. Through belly-down play in the first months of life, your little one is calibrating her understanding of her head position. She learns through her eyes and inner ears to orient upright. Any neck asymmetries can negatively impact this development and should be remedied as soon as possible. Carefully observe your baby in Tummy Time and watch for any consistent head tilting in one direction or any strong preferences for looking only one direction. Strategically place photos and toys to encourage looking in all directions to help your kiddo strengthen out of any asymmetries. Discuss any concerns with your child's pediatrician for further evaluation.

BENEFITS: spinal development, neck strength, upper body strength, core strength, movement sense, visual sense, eye movement skills, attention, pressure & stretch sense, body awareness, stretch & strengthen out of womb position, prevent Flat Head Syndrome

BLANKET HAMMOCK

Your newborn's developing sensory systems and her connection to you help give her a sense of security and well-being in the face of new experiences. One fun new movement experience is to have two adults hold opposite corners of your baby's blanket to lift her up into a hammock for swinging and gentle bouncing. Begin with your baby's blanket on a bed. Place baby on her back on the blanket and lift the corners with a partner. Keeping the blanket over the bed for safety, swing baby side to side and head to toe. Lift the blanket high and low. Vary the speed and intensity of your movements and watch your infant's reactions.

The pressure of different parts of her body pressing into the blanket as her weight shifts helps your newborn learn to orient and respond to movement based on her pressure & stretch sense. This is an important building block to the development of balance.

BENEFITS: movement sense, touch sense, pressure & stretch sense, visual sense, body awareness, balance, socialization & bonding

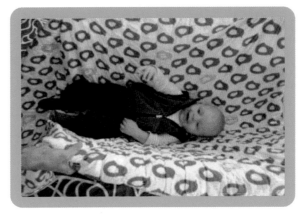

BALL ROLLING ON BODY

Your baby gains valuable body awareness through touch and pressure from the world around him. Feeling sensation in his own body is an important component of early play. A simple game to capitalize on your baby's interest in touch sensations is to roll a soft ball over his body parts. Trace an outline of his body as he lays on the floor. Roll a ball over his back and down his legs in Tummy Time. Gently bounce the ball on his arms and hands.

Naming body parts is an early language skill that you can foster with this game. Playtime is the perfect time to get talking, get silly and enjoy your baby!

BENEFITS: movement sense, touch sense, pressure & stretch sense, visual sense, body awareness, balance, socialization & bonding

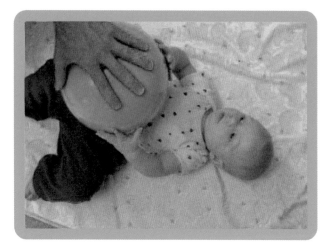

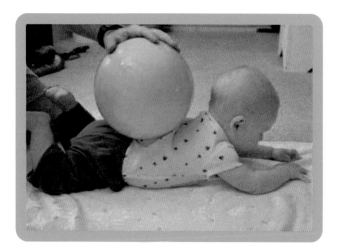

GRABBING BASKETS

When she first starts opening and closing her hands, your baby won't be very effective at grasping but her attempts to secure objects will strengthen her hand muscles, improve her coordination, and capture her attention.

As she's learning to grasp, your baby will be most successful with lightweight toys that can be secured with lots of different hand and finger positions. By placing objects in a basket or small shallow pan, you allow baby to push and bump her hands up against items while keeping them close. She can also use the wall of the container to help her grasp the items. Cut paper towel or toilet paper tubes make great early grasp toys. Cut them into rings about 1-2" wide and place them in a low basket or pan. Ribbon strips are easy grasping toys. Golf balls, when too big to grasp, make a great noise when placed in a metal pan and pushed around. Your baby is too young for ring stacker or shape sorter toys but you can place the pieces in a grabbing basket. Position baby seated on your lap or belly-down over a pillow to free her hands for grasping.

BENEFITS: sense of touch, coordination of reach, grasping skills, visual skills, body awareness, attention, bring hands together, spinal development, pressure & stretch sense, upper body strength, core strength, neck strength, prevent Flat Head Syndrome

HERB SCENTED GRABBING TOYS

Soft objects make great early grasping toys but you don't need dozens of stuffed animals for your little one. Make scented grabbing toys from baby socks for a great grabbing activity that uses multiple senses. Simply fill clean baby socks with fresh herbs such as rosemary and mint. Pair two baby socks and fold their tops over to make a soft packet. Place baby seated on your lap or belly-down over a Tummy Time pillow for grabbing play.

As always, closely supervise your baby during play. This means eyes on baby within arm's reach.

BENEFITS: sense of touch, visual sense, sense of smell, coordination of reach, grasping skills

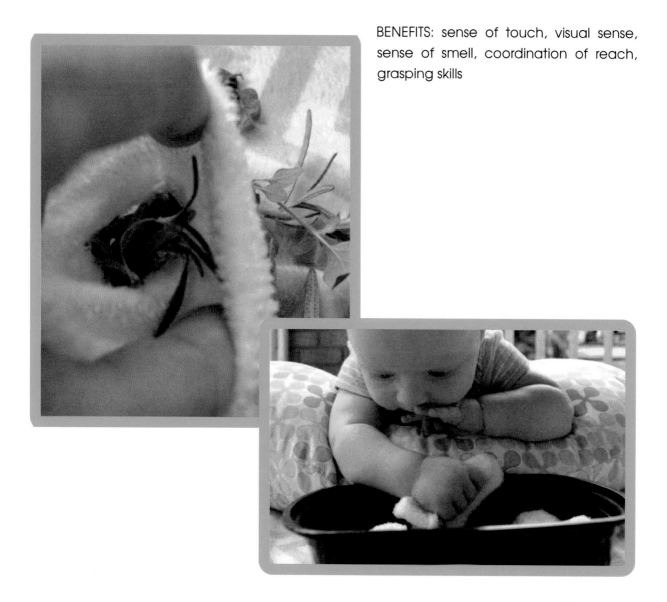

HANGING TEETHER TOYS

In month four, hands aren't the only thing opening and closing on toys. Your newborn's mouth is getting more and more interested in exploring, too. Your baby may be able to briefly hold a toy placed in his hands but likely drops it before he's able to mouth it successfully. Help your little one get the oral input he craves by hanging teether toys from his activity gym. Use ribbons or plastic toy links to secure toys at a height that reaches your infant's mouth. Watch for his hands to come up to his mouth and attempt to grasp and hold his toys -the same skill that will help him hold a bottle or cup in the months ahead.

Oral play can be drooly but it's an important developmental step that readies your baby's mouth for eating and talking. He gains awareness of his tongue, cheeks, and gums. The input stimulates him to move and strengthen these body parts. In addition, he experiences textures and shapes with his mouth just like he does when playing with his hands. This helps him learn about objects in the world around him.

BENEFITS: sense of touch, pressure & stretch sense, body awareness, mouth coordination, speech, grasping skills, coordination of reach, hand strength, bringing hands together, attention, visual sense

A GLITTER JAR

Now that your infant is able to support his weight and keep his head up in Tummy Time, he may begin to reach out to touch objects in this position. This marks huge developments in strength, sensory processing, and motor planning. Your little one must shift his weight onto one arm and balance while planning and executing a reach with the other arm.

One activity to capitalize on your baby's innate interest in reaching is to make a simple cause and effect toy - a glitter jar. Fill an empty plastic bottle or glass jar with water, 1 tbsp of glycerine (from your craft store or pharmacy), and glitter. You can spice things up with foil confetti or other lightweight objects to float in your baby's glitter jar. Shake the jar and place it in front of your little one in Tummy Time. Begin with rolling the container on its side and as your baby gets better able to reach, place it upright to knock down. Show your baby how moving the jar stirs up the glitter. Through repetition, he'll begin to associate the action with the result. Cause and effect play will capture your newborn's attention for months to come - glitter jars are just the beginning!

BENEFITS: visual sense, coordination of reach, neck strength, core strength, upper body strength, balance, prevent Flat Head Syndrome, attention, body awareness, spinal development, pressure & stretch sense

SIDE TO SIDE ROLLING

Movement is play for babies. Simple newborn movement games help your child discover, explore, and learn about himself and his surroundings. You can help your baby enjoy the rocking sensations of

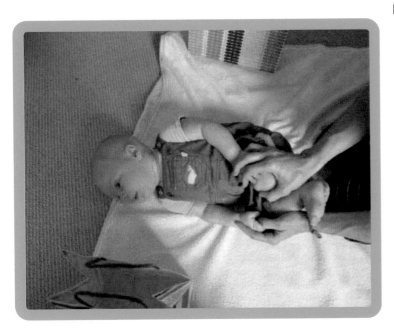

rolling side to side on his blanket even before he's rolling on his own. This will give his pressure & stretch sense and movement sense lots of important information about his body position related to the ground beneath him and to gravity.

With baby on his back, guide his hands to his knees or feet. Gently and slowly rock him side to side as you sing or talk. Place toys, gift bags, or other interesting sights on either side for your little one to see as he moves back and forth.

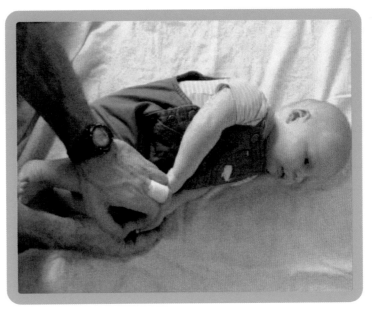

BENEFITS: sense of touch, pressure & stretch sense, movement sense, balance, visual sense, body awareness, prevent Flat Head Syndrome, socialization & bonding, speech

A STREAMER FAN

Your little one is fast becoming a Tummy Time pro - lifting her head higher and for longer. Give her the chance to practice head turning and weight shifting in Tummy Time with an oscillating streamer fan. Tape streamers or ribbons to an oscillating fan and place your kiddo belly-down several feet in front. Turn the fan to low and watch your baby follow the movement and feel the breeze pass by.

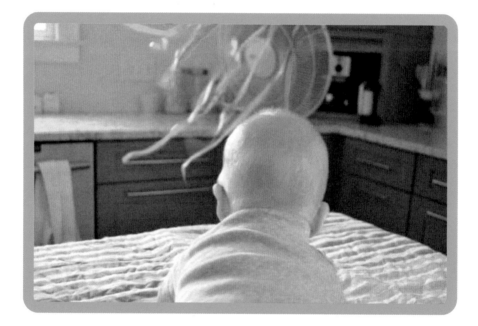

Early newborn learning centers around noticing patterns - things that happen repeatedly and predictably. Your little one will watch and soon discover that the breeze blowing on her face is related to the fan passing by. In addition to the physical benefits of this activity, your baby will use her curiosity, attention, and observation skills to learn!

BENEFITS: visual sense, eye movement skills, sense of touch, pressure & stretch sense, spinal development, body awareness, attention, stretch & strengthen out of womb position, prevent Flat Head Syndrome, upper body strength, core strength, neck strength

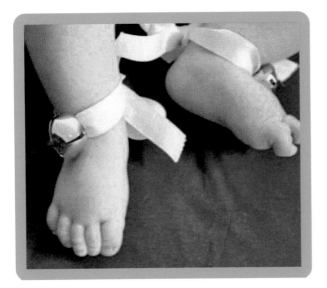 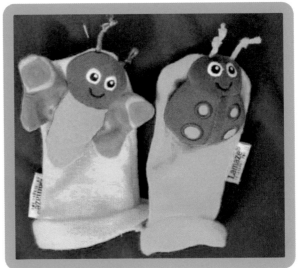

FOOT RATTLES

Adding the sound of bells or rattles to your infant's feet in weeks 13-16 taps into his growing interest in his lower body and encourages him to reach for his feet. This is important for developing the belly and leg strength and body awareness for a fast approaching motor milestone - the "4 month roll".

Your little one will begin to curl up in a ball while on his back and roll to one side. He'll then stretch out and lift his head to complete the roll onto his tummy. But your baby has been preparing since his first week for this accomplishment. Giving him plenty of floortime play on his blanket has allowed him to stretch, strengthen, gain awareness of his body in relation to the ground beneath him and gravity, and to practice the movements that make up the 4 month roll. Simple play activities like tying bells to your infant's ankles or putting on sock rattles contribute to his healthy sensory, motor and cognitive development.

BENEFITS: movement sense, touch sense, pressure & stretch sense, visual sense, body awareness, balance, socialization & bonding

RIBBON GRABBING GAME

In recent weeks, your kiddo has practiced opening and closing his hands and developing his sense of touch by exploring objects. When you begin to see him open and close to grasp intentionally, a whole world of play opportunities opens up. A fun, simple grasping activity to try with your little one is a Ribbon Grabbing game.

Drape ribbon strips over your baby's activity gym and place baby belly-up underneath. Closely supervise as your baby touches, bats at and begins to grab and pull the ribbons down. Make sure your baby doesn't roll or get tangled in the ribbons. Watch as he explores and enjoys his new grabbing skills.

BENEFITS: grasping skills, coordination of reach, hand strength, upper body strength, sense of touch, pressure & stretch sense, bringing hands together, stretch & strengthen out of womb position, body awareness, attention

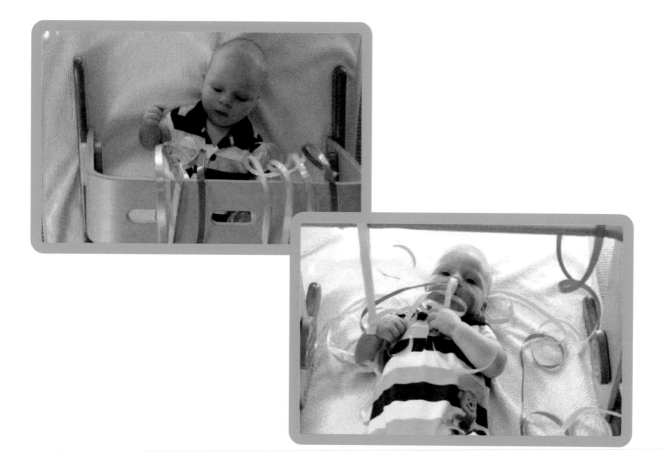

GLOSSARY OF KEY TERMS

Baby Holding Devices : any positioner that supports baby in a semi-reclined position including car seat carriers used outside of the car, infant swings, rock & play seats, bouncy seats, foam napping wedges & sleeper seats, infant lounge pillows,

Pressure & Stretch Sense : Proprioceptive Sense

Movement Sense : Vestibular Sense

Sense of Touch : Tactile Sense

Hearing Sense : Auditory Sense

Eye Movement Skills : Ocular Motor Skills

Flat Head Syndrome : Positional Plagiocephaly

Coordination of Reach : Visual Motor Skills

Using Two Hands Together : Bilateral Coordination

Mouth Coordination : Oral Motor Skills

Spinal Development : the progression from the C-shaped spine of the fetal position to the S-shaped spine of an adult through the development of cervical and lumbar spinal curves

RELATED RESEARCH

Abbott AL, Bartlett DJ. Infant motor development and equipment use in the home. *Child: Care Health & Development.* 2001: 27: 295-306.

American Physical Therapy Association. Lack of time on tummy shown to hinder achievement of developmental milestones, say physical therapist. News Release. 2008; August 6, 2008

Batlett DJ, Kneale Fanning JE. Relationships of equipment use and play positions to motor development at eight months corrected age of infants born preterm. *Pediatric Physical Therapy.* 2003; 15: 8-15

Hotelling BA. Tools for teaching - newborn capabilities: parent teaching is a necessity. *The Journal of Perinatal Education.* 2004; 13(4): 43-49.

Pin T, Eldridge B and Galea MP. A review of the effects of sleep position, play position and equipment use on motor development of infants. Development Medicine and Child Neurology. 2007; 49: 858-867

Hutchinson L, THomspon J, Mitchell E. Determinants of nonsynostotic plagiocephaly: A case-control study. Pediatrics. 2003; 112(4): 316-322

Persing J, James H, Swanson J, Kattwinkel J. Committee onPractice and Ambulatory Medicine, Section on Plastic Surgery & Section on Neurological Surgery. Prevention and management of positional skull deformities in infants. *Pediatrics.* 2003; 112(1): 199-202.

Van Vlimmeren LA, Helders PJM, Van Adrichem AV, Engelbert, RHH. Torticollis and plagiocephaly in infancy: therapeutic strategies. *Pediatric Rehabilitiation* 2006: 9(1): 40-46.

Made in the USA
San Bernardino, CA
05 July 2020